THE REPOETIC: AFTER SAINT–POL–ROUX

Benjamin C. Dugdale

Guelph, Ontario

Edited by Shane Neilson
Cover and book design by Jeremy Luke Hill
Cover image by Ryan Heshka
Proofreading by Sheri Doyle
Set in PingFang and Centaur
Printed on Mohawk Via Felt
Printed and bound by Arkay Design & Print

LIBRARY AND ARCHIVES CANADA CATALOGUING IN PUBLICATION

Title: The repoetic : after Saint-Pol-Roux / Benjamin C. Dugdale.
Names: Dugdale, Benjamin C., author. | Saint-Pol-Roux, 1861-1940. Répoétique.
Description: Poems.
Identifiers: Canadiana (print) 20220481113 | Canadiana (ebook) 20220481148 |
    ISBN 9781774220733 (softcover) | ISBN 9781774220740 (PDF) |
    ISBN 9781774220757 (EPUB)
Classification: LCC PS8607.U375985 R37 2023 | DDC C811/.6—dc23

Gordon Hill Press gratefully acknowledges the support of the Canada Council for the Arts, the Ontario Arts Council, and the Ontario Book Tax Publishing Credit.

Gordon Hill Press respectfully acknowledges the ancestral homelands of the Attawandaron, Anishinaabe, Haudenosaunee, and Métis Peoples, and recognizes that we are situated on Treaty 3 territory, the traditional territory of Mississaugas of the Credit First Nation.

Gordon Hill Press also recognizes and supports the diverse persons who make up its community, regardless of race, age, culture, ability, ethnicity, nationality, gender identity and expression, sexual orientation, marital status, religious affiliation, and socioeconomic status.

Gordon Hill Press
130 Dublin Street North
Guelph, Ontario, Canada
N1H 4N4
www.gordonhillpress.com

This poem is dedicated first and foremost to Jane, my "stubborn mother who simply *can't. be. killed*"; may you live forever.

With special note of love to Olivia, Drake, and Mason. As Yo La Tengo promises, "You can have it all."

Table of Contents

1. Mortar/Morte err umm

∴

The soy-slick throat uncooperative as a candied saltlick
The battery-drain brain clogged so bad the heart-garburator can't start

∴

The sidereal taxidermmensity
fanfaronadic fanfic with the posture of ultimatum
how to grasp The Repoetic other than like a plummeting lover
        you know
        the kind you just met on Tinder
        who wants you to be *their person*

The gum-got hair of the wanting to find the bust Repoetic
        this barnacle-bloom spireality all day-glo long tongue

You and the Tinder-Poem in the mirror brush your teeth together and think
about what it
        would mean to cum on the fire in the fireplace so hard you doused it
        (and not just because Saint-Pol-Roux suggested)

        then after, to fire on the cum in the cumplace so hard you 'gain roused it

^Stair cas~ing~ into it, wondering if that rash (decision, with the person, fri[ss/cti]on)
was going to Mountain Dew to you what you feared it ought2

That Saint_Pol_Roux.avi, dead of heartbreak, abandoned the anti-Republic
that the bedded Word will only bend so far to make The Repoetic real to
make ends meet as meat ends mend each sweet leech-like hickey-seal breach

The Tinder-Poem the cum-whorl of the tenement building's shared first-
floor hot-tub

∴

Woendering whither my trundle thru the hessian threshold of the demi-ruins
of the unrealized Repoetic — like I were the Angelic FemmeBoyHooters
head cheerleader in the Word's pep-rally and the bust-thru jute banner
was an unhooked rug — if my having known German and a bit of Danish
disqualified me or brought little toxic translation barbs in an ech/o/h no of
that whole nastiness where a soused German Soldat wandered in to the house
and shot (to death) governess, Rose, and shot (but not to death) daughter,
Divine, but fled finally at the bark of a dog, Who Knows, and then later on
someone else broke in again and burned most of the manuscripts and art and
so self-Sainted Saint-Pol-Roux died of his broken heart

It's out of the way now
Why does verb sproing into Word when you translate it
Wondering about this phoront asleep in the matted hammock of historhair
        the French in the language my idiot brain-damage'd brain groomed
        into my aerated English,
        my *Nu-Cue-Ler* Alberta English, my used-to-be-the-bottom-of-an-
        Ocean English

        (do you remember being taught as a child that paper
        was our primary non-renewable resource too? just us?)

Wondering how The Repoetic is still washing up on the winter-salt scuffed
        jean cuffs at the sure-thing
        south-shore shore-whorl of Ratlantis that I the Idiot-Emeritus of the
        Republic had thought I'd been the first to discover

Sipping my mocktail hot toddy (hot to-do-list, an essential given my brain-
        tamping err umm
        brain-damage) thru the fibrils of the gnawed plastic *nuh-uh* straw

∴

This is the part where the intelligent poet who doesn't hate The Republic in the way the Idiot-Emeritus does—which is to say as a passionate child with nothing to lose and having never lost yet—cites a few poets on how to write, maybe Phil Hall name-dropping some dead poets he was buddies with [geeze, I am so young when compared, tho' many of my beloved are wormdirt too; autocorrect tossing *geese* int(uit/o) the ring, ushering me to an ill/poly/g(l) ot CanLit GG not so subtly]; maybe Shannon Maguire talking about Giorgio Agamben but actually talking about an ambulating exploded sestina but actually it's all ants and I think I've got a pretty strong argument that *gender* and *gardener* cannot be untangled by Pepsi-Challenge mouth-feel, especially while they're still stuck in Maguire's generous garburator-ing poem-thing (oh were we so lucky); maybe ask the poets to pipe down so I can listen for the Pied Piper luring all these shore-lorn pile-bits up Potato Beach to the tune of Inspector Gadget; Attirer toutes ces ruines de châteaux sur la plage de Apple of the Berth Beach avec un air d'encouragement; err, umm

the Verb—yeah, I'll choo-choo [cab/ch]oose to make it that instead of the Word, even if it's a verb the way slipping and falling to your knees with a kneecap slipping free (Liberty! oh I've translated it enough times I'm recognizing it at a second glance) while pushing a Firebird out from a very small and unassuming snow pile is, a neighbour's firebird, the kind with the feature that tells you when to shift, because sometimes when you're a young woman learning to drive stick for the first time in an affordable vehicle like a Firebird (what a name for a car I mean come'on and it's not even the name of an Indigenous nation we're [see:settlers] desperate to ossify by means of...) is a great rig to learn on and it tells you when to shift even, a verb that is spinning bald tires in the Pill-Hill parking lot while all the filth of the car-topia rears back and kicks you donkey-like—taking on the strain of a stain, not a tint, but a stain, and maybe the intelligent Tinder-Poem perks up here with a textiles essay but in case it doesn't I mean (I, mean, title of my memoir amirite) it the way the angry child thrashes on the winter beach & smears juice the thiccosity of menstrual blood across its cheek and smiles as wide as a dog in the Hortons Drivethru while I'm waiting on my doubledouble étoile and trouble double-dog-dared plain timbit boon; yeah, yeah he's cute, yeah, he's a boy, yeah, yeah, no, I've never met another dog named Bacchus either, yeah no for sure.

∴

I took Coke at the Pepsi Challenge

∴

It was a Sunfire not a Firebird
And while Sunfire is not appropriated
Pontiac is
When you slap your forehead involuntarily you make your immortal mother
mad
(but try telling that to the sprung rat trap of muscle memory, to void-
warranty masculinity)
Damage damage damage
The Repoetic ever-unbuilding, un$_{rolled}$ un$_{hooked}$ rug
A firepit off a low-bowl veranda
The black-licked bricks Chiclets kicked inward
In a word
A fire *place*
Fallen in on itself
Redundant
Not Firebird (aka Phoenix aka rebirdth moteef)
Repundant
Sunfire
Sun is a fire *place*
Perhaps *the* fire *place* to end all fire places

Lawnbandoned litter, child-sized sour-blue vampire fangs
Golden hour greens them up a lickle   so very there   like a bear trap

Hidden in the den with the hotwaterbottle-NRE radiating
from your burlfriend's lap, trick of the eye, fib rill fibrils
redund   ant exploding sestina all ambu[r]lating

∴

Redun (capital D) D-esire
D-sire the melancholic spiral, like soft-reset it, vampire style; tiny fang in tiny
    center-hole to rewire the
    factory settings
    woendering into the thought that a Vampire is the loneliest creature
    because they live forever and always want and only want what's bad for
    the rest of us (Salem's) lot
    woendering so hard my knit brow looks like the Buffy Vampire brows

But of course D-spite all my own woenliness I'm out there thinking that in
    the sun

The Sun's potluck the sunD-ry starloaf out on the picnic table
    Us all lamenting Mayor Homolka's re-election in Toront/o/h no
    Plat/o/h no praising the "practical gesture" in a press-release:

    "I'm pretty sure she's not a poet so it's cool (thumbs up emoji/tongue
    out emoji)"

∴

All those hermaphroditic PoemAngels S-P-R whorlshipped
What would Saint-Pol-Roux think of Vivian Girls
What would Saint-Pol-Roux think of ContraPoints
What would Saint-Pol-Roux think of Elliot Page or *Juno* in the context of
Elliot Page
Though we do know Saint-Pol-Roux would worship Lady
FemmeBoyHooter
(it's spelt different
'cause it's fancier)
(we know from context-clues, specifically bulk-laundry receipts)

∴

Cork Jester plugged up with stifled laughter at a DM/eme from her Tinder-
    Poem S.O.
Chose-Coke poser (the speaker) from Pepsi mouth-feel challenge thinking
    aloud about her(d) Alberda-English, Plato Play-Doh in'r moudf, the
    poem prying open those girly wights

That melancholy fang in yr neck(st of kin) again
Thrall-crawl along the mall's thoroughfare
    all along the blacklight bowling alley
    glass-blowing artery

    all the food-court Churro you could dream of
The Repoetic reconstituted in a food-tray fastness
    you and your friends forever in love in a booth
    eating whatever we want and eating together forever

    the saptack snack-attack derailed by a glimpse of the capital B B-eauty
    the FemmeBoyHooters Angel coming to bus the B-ooth
    B-eww ty-svm

    the Pipsay stain across brusque coroner's mouth-corner
    booth across from us
    with the ornery judge in the corduroy coveralls

    Grace Jones in a powdered wig
    how'd she end up with that gig?

the fastness taking on the posture of coroner's curt whisper
Grace Jones intoning laws and all the things The Repoetic was supposed to be
    free from

Dam it
Cork Gesture, plz

∴

Tinder-Poem lit the litter of well wishes
        the snowsumed forget-got barley in the distance a-shiver
Thunder blender-blunder, no lid, bent blades vavvooming up blent liquid
that is the unstable
        tornado that is The Repoetic (that is the "that is the" umm/ah-like
        utterance of the Verb's atomic gust)

I lan/d/izzy, islandized, turvy in the pwrbttm waddle every enby cattle
hunter recognized from twenty acres off

                                                        a report
old as a dead star we hang our newborn poems on
the stretched elastic embouchure of the things I want to say, cannot couch-
twirl thru the
        threshold

exhausted, the 'lastic lapsed to a horseshoe
a glass horseshoe for Tinder-Poem's perfect tabi-toes

∴

A bale's-worth baleful drone
The Repoetic's lone cathedral cast-iron bell
Castaway on the sheep-shorn wool-snow southern shore
Its uvula banging the inside of its sand-sealed mouth
"Let me out, let me out"
Its pout flash-mobbing out sonar-sandcast
Snow interpolating sand
Shore interpolating land
Slimy timey-wimey oneness

The Angelic Hootermaphrodite S_P_R.avi sung of
Prepared-piano #3 for 100 Snow-Blowers, Concert C

∴

The shift-indicator noticed only now, beaming like a toothless child's smile, the dog nursing the Timbit like a newborn on the lap of the Tinder-Poem riding shotgun, clinking its glass horseshoe slippers together to the tune of Tubular Bells

∴

The Repoetic
The place where bird on fire lays les œufs du futur
somewhere in the knock-off [Pr/D]ada clutch, the inheritor Poet blare-apparent

That brain-tumour what made a puppet of my mother on about:
With yer sisters I never had heartburn, and they were born without eyebrows
But you, you hairy baby, all heartburn all day
Could barely keep my Coca-Cola down

Now most of that brain-tumour in whatever stands in for a firepit in a hospital
        Not just us hicks burning our garbage, the doctors that do all the
        death-doing Mountain
                Dew'ing it too
That tumor and its cousins, many unclaimed medi-mementos now furnace-
        flung ash at the
        unfurnished open-house of the sky that's just waiting to be blotted out
        by a Repoetician
                skyline

The oracular Gecko fused to the broiling inner-Chiclets-brick, fuelled by
        burnt elegiac
        manuscripts for the stubborn mother who simply can't. be. killed.

A relief of on two front teef, the shadow of a cold-blooded peeping vertebrate

The nervous Tinder-Poem thinquiring
                "does your English always fight like this, or just at the holidays?"

2. Demesne, Cryptoportique

"This process, of course, made my translation 'false' to some, while it is still
irrevocably a translation, but to an exorbitance. Exorbitant happenstance.
Exstance. Extantiation. A performative gesture altering space,
altering the original, and altering my own voice and capacity in English.
All of which is, I think, the best that translation can do."

—Erín Moure, "The Exhorbitant Body: Translation As Performance"

"…does the citizen of a republic, occupy space—i.e., bespeak sense
differently [+ by differently I do not mean better] in the 'same' English
language, than, say, the subject of a former Dominion?"

—Gail Scott, "The Sutured Subject"

∴

Way of entry:
Affix the provided pocket-mirror within your mouth
Then find the reflecting pool
If the pocket mirror is whelmed with your clotted splendor you may enter

∴

The aged baker's backacre acreage full of dinosaur bones repatriated to the earth after dism antling the Philosopher King's ill-got throne one overt rhyming couplet at a time

The land is the Verb
Not land as in lain and known laneway
Land as in
Return to earth after leap

∴

When we speak of Earthly
We mean *earthly* in the way critics described all Rock Hudson's Sirk roles
As in the earth is a beloved faggot as well
It too watches the death of whole generations of those it loves, it too will
wither and blink out one day of heartbreak because when everyone you love
is sick you are sick too; making it into the house before the door closes and
the frost sets in means you alone wil[l/t] from the window, all the warmth
up in the cupola, "out of my hands" it says, thinning and grinning into
neoliberal nothingness

The Earth gives its earthly thumbs up to the environmental impact assessment
for the permits to build The Repoetic on so-called "Crown Land"

∴

The Repoetic is not a MoralMost- or Merit- ocracy,
Social media is a redundancy here
Where we all lead the lives we wish we could
Where we all share in the "public" living as much or as little as we desire
No one is damned for feeling down
For not smiling wide enough at "it could be worse, you could be dead"
Suffering is still relative, but all of it is valid
There's no law to pour our anxieties into the mold of, though we do cast
many many decoys of deceased pets and nubile nuisible anime body-pillows

If you're wondering WHERE we are
it's the same state *The Simpsons* takes place in

The Jedi have no place here but the prequels are screened on the quack-grass
slope every
      Sunday, except the first and last, when the Swans come in and do what
      swans do, all neck and no quarter

∴

Mara Jade-d

The consequence for me reading *Fanged Noumena* as an ironic bit I couldn't quit was becoming the bullseye target for a UR prof, Dr. Formal (née D.Hyde), who daily workshopped an unpublished "12 Rules…" rebuttal bulletpoint list derived from the Discworld works of Terry Pratchett and who threatened to beat up Jordan Peterson in the parking lot after school (but neither one of them showed up for the fight). I suppose I hadn't been loud enough when I scarified *I'm not a boy* into my left cheek o'er the bathroom break. The consequence for scarifying *I'm not a boy* with a clicky-pencil's tiny tip on my left cheek was that Doc watched me the whole time in the mirror from the urinal and so to him my declaration came out backwards: *I'm a boy, bruh.*

Dude, he's asking me, and for no good reason not asking the rest of Briar Rose's Dozen Grad-goons, *but what if rule four was straight up just magic? And six was centrist bootlick?* And then he beat me black and blue-milk in the parking lot with my 86-page "Phorontology: Crystal Vampires across the Star Wars Continuity Can(y)on" final research paper, (which he'd pushed me to redirect my attention to when he turned down my proposal to write on Simpsons "FFWD Futurity"). And then I gave him my lunch money for a flash drive full of pirated literary theory he'd never read. And then he beat me up again in the parking lot to workshop it, a tenured bit. I wonder if *what's playing him* understands corpse-camping is a dink move.

The consequence from scarifying myself to remind him what I amn't was it came out in italics, and for that he beat me doubly with my tea-stained copy of *Dubliners* in the parking lot—but not, he insisted, for shortening his name to *Doc Dickhead* from Doctor *GalaxyBrain, Checkmate Fascists*—one kick for each of the I 3 5 0 0 0 dollars he earns annually to crowdsource "12 Rules by Terry Pratchett (RIP) [by Doctor GalaxyBrain, Checkmate Fascists]" rebuttal bullet points from his skeletal keening grad students.

The consequence to the cheek-cut cum-outing was girl talk around the water cooler on our second 15, cooler unspun and giving glugglug grief like a sputtering lightbulb and me stumbling onto the scene and

getting doused wet khakis-ed. The consequence of the carceral lightbulb
moment was I went back to the land to quote dickhead late-life Nick
Land, but I forgot my lighter and my ultimate tent pegging compilations.

The consequence of my willingly illiterate prof 'rehabilitating'
humanism (and, according to him, all by his lonesome) was I didn't
fall under that rehabilitated humanist cumbrella; Yum, yee-ha. *A girl
with glasses, she looks / real smart, just looked* back at me in the pocket mirror
of my mouth. The problem with the impossible mirror 'Contact' shot
is I s(woosh)unk it from the they/thy/them/thee-point line, and the
consequence of some day-dreamt carnal contact was me reading *Fanged
Noumena* as an ironic bit I couldn't quit.

I edited the callout post from *Lizard Ppl of Eden* to *(W)izard Ppl of
Eden* under advisement from an emotional terrorist in the interest of not
scarifying a bullseye on my ass-cheek (they were right, but for the wrong
reasons),   and on the next season of umbra bedlam: James Dean
leaning life-size in the Tinder-Poem's long body-mirror reaching out to
tenderly knuckleback my untouched right cheek, and it'd be okay bcs Roy
Orbison was gonna tutor me in anything I want, specifically machine-
learning,

and I was there, looking at a *girl with glasses*, yearning, crypto$-earning.

∴

The newel-born spiral cosmic muchness closer now than e'er before
The clerestorial frost crackling with the slow southerly slide of piped
    cholesterol dollops
     a whistle out of sight so sh rill it cuts the mountains twain-cloud loud

∴

Tag yrself: yr "canada beef inc"
im "misand, hold the ry"
I wanted to be "canada beef" twin too, but didn't want to double up
It's very sweet of you to say "that's ok theres plenty of room for cowgirls in alberta"
I took a dark blue sharpie to the still damp drywall of The Repoetic and wrote down
        "there's plenty of room for cowgirls in Alberta"
In The Repoetic The Simpsons *is always on in the background and today it's* Barthood
the Boyhood *parody and Milhouse is getting ready for college and he's telling everyone how he'll
reinvent himself and pretend he has a canadian girlfriend from Alberta and she's named Alberta too
so he has less lies to keep track of*
Yes, one day I too could be that imaginary Albertan cowgirl girlfriend, Alberta

Alberta? More like Allberta.

3. Tremblevator

"…if you were a plumber and wrote beautiful, insightful essays which were read by a community of twenty people—twenty *real* readers—would that work for you? If not, why not? Philip Glass was a plumber."

—B.D. McClay, "Loser Theory"

∴

The pseudobezoar, we should've told you before, was the tin likeness of the
       entirety of the
       world, history included
But what's swallowed is swallowed, yano
The union would do something but they're trying not to get involved with the
       Coca-Coalition
Let the magpies do the thinking a little while

The Carnassial Night 'bout to bite

Polishing a flame to sterility
Sun ever-guttering, gargling
(garburator garburator-ing
soft-gold crown o'PhilKing)

The Repoetic always undoing itself in ant icipation of this great, opalhessi ant
       fraying

20.
Dynamit R0LL
$ 11.95

∴

Not a lot of writers have moved in here yet
It's way too quiet
A lot of comic book artist refugees though
Something magic about being able to draw a thing that you can pause, or
nest in another thing, and all those things can exist without talking to explain
themselves, so binding, and of course a couple of the educated monied
poets have been complaining loudly about that to me, but I'm just the Baron
Administrator; I can't do anything to make the comic book panels that show
you ennui&melancholy & make you sit with them without making a punchline
of them, I can't do anything to make them less *popular* nor *effective* than poems
that trot out candied jargon that doesn't understand the theory it's p[irate]
[arroting] from ten years ago that all the other disciplines already abandoned

The birdgeoisie seem to be enjoying themselves as they pencil in their nature
journals, something something runnel, the vicious swans making boy rubble
of their troubling boy bodies, going quiet and quick into the SwanGullets

It's all satin lotsness ooh bb yes blurrrrry

Most of the poets keep trying to matte-pat down their sprung Alfalfa hair nodes

It's like they don't get what The Repoetic can do for everyone

∴

Tinder-Poem fidget puckeruining loop by loop all night
an ant ique hooked rug, Green on White:

D   o   n   '   t
S   p   i   t   !

What once was housemaker's decree
Now a tender dare, composed just for me

"You're laughing too loud aloud"
Someone asking Tinder-Poem just *what* they thought they were
& hoo Tinder-Poem thought I was too

"Wh[o/at] am I?
I'm the B I T C H you hear
When you say obituary out loud
As in yerrrs, if you don't mind yer gob"

And I'm that too, but with *Bitumen*   :/

But I'd rather not admit it
so cozy here in my rot-got fleece blankey
this expressly unwashed nest
in my hidey corner of the crowddead hysplex

∴

The Swans are starting to cause a little more trouble than we ant icipated
30-50 feral Swans "deterritorialized" our Poem-State "without organs," as in
     they've been wringing our
     first-person-plural neck with our freshly eviscerated guts
The foothills are alive with goose flesh and we insist anyone going out for a
     stroll buddy up, and if they must go it alone, be aware: don't wear yr
     headphones

FemmeBoy Broidery abode no terrors
Tho' it wilted and came undone
As The Repoetic is obliged to

∴

"What're you getting up to for the day?"

"I think I'm just gonna do some reading, take some notes."

The Tinder-Poem a striking figure sitting at the end the bed, adjusts its near-sheer knickers, snickers at the freshly hung dry-cleaning shimmer: "this suit used to belong to Waylon Smithers, but before that, Judy Garland. That was after he was briefly black."

I utter the sacrostudy's passwhorld to the unseen bouncer, a tired old joke. "'My pronouns are:
Girl Wedged Under The Front Of A Firebird /
Girl Wedged Under The Front Of A Sunfire.'"

Entry. The sacrostudy so stuffy. Leather desktop receptive to my thumb-drumming nonsense.

Many rare books I'm afraid to touch on the highest shelf I can't reach anyhow:

Tuck Your Penis by Ms Points; *The Type-Face History of The Necronomicon* in a special one-off goat-flesh binding from Gaspereau Press; an unabridged paperback copy of *The Story of the Vivian Girls, in What Is Known as the Realms of the Unreal, of the Glandeco-Angelinian War Storm, Caused by the Child Slave Rebellion* by H. Darger (small enough to fit in your pocket); *The Angry Dad Omnibus* by B. Simpson; Extremely Rare Var. Cover *Sad Girl #1* (VF/NM) by L. Simpson (Illustrated M. Simpson); *DC Elseworlds presents: Roxie The Street Shark*; a first edition *My Mother Taught Me* by Tor Kung; Routledge's *Bobblehead Dashboard Figurines Through the Age*s; every issue of *Die Freundin* (untranslated); several sun-kissed copies of *14 Poets* (it came out just before all the other nonsense, and there was, mercifully, no mention of Atwood at all, as though she'd never existed in the first place); and one of *t)here: the other* other *Canadian poetrie*s.

Free at last, wincing from the ruth of fresh air.

I watched unseen, yet unspoken and unthought-of in my own private way, as
      the philosophy club looked out over the vista of the Mountain Dew-
      green dill glen and the thousand plateaus, and I saw them look up to
      see the Mountain Dew-yellow prescription bottle and its peeling sticker
      bingo-blotting out the hobgoblin sun on the horizon:
      N
      O
      R
      E
      F
      I
      L
      L
      S

∴

The boîte à suggestion has been full lately and we get it
Winter in The Repoetic is no picnic
I too nightly find my jeans diamond with flashlit flurry
Would you rather choke in the city ???
Such is the price of solitude

And yes
We've heard of the hauntings
We don't think we need to take money from the pool for "I drink my ginger ale can completely and leave it on the night stand and when I wake up there's always a new fresh gulp in the bottom" because, like, that seems like a good and miraculous thing? Are we reading the room wrong? And are you sure you drink the whole thing each time? And do you really drink an entire Canada Dry _{right} before bed every night? Sorry, Sussex Ginger Ale?

∴

Yes I have been caught with my bindle wet with grief as a twilit silhouette
As I am not an elected official this is no scandal; this bindle bears no shame

∴

And if I catch another fucking one of you running your mouth about how "cringe" it was when the FemmeBoy AngelSong of the ApocEllipsis high5d the Tinder-Poem after the two of them successfully navigated the nauseatingly sterile and embarrassing Weed Store for the first time because neither of them grew up in households where they would have had the spare income or privacy or hippy-parental encouragement to try drugs at that age, I swear to fucking Verb!!!

Chose-Coke poser and the Tinder-Poem were bad at being *non-biney le-dollar-beans* because they didn't U-Haul, nor were they interminably chill (on social media nor irl); one had a cat, the other a dog, and both snored like they were their own fathers; it was nice to have your own hidey-hole hole-in-the-wall, your own entropic laundry pile as testament to uninsured and thus unmedicated depression; pet-sitters and sleepovers could always be arranged.

They did live next to one another though in The Repoetic's lone chopped-up Earl-liquidated mansion cum apartment complex (which the many 'burb blurbers were desperate to re-zone into death-throes), and all that separated them was a scab of ever-damp drywall and the seafoam transom.

Translots, more like, Tinder-Poem thot.

∴

Marilyn Gorgonroe, Bane of Snack-Seekers and Slushy-Sluts Alike, will sell
    you single smokes if you add yourself to her Poem-A-Day mailing list

Cross-legged in a tangle together
We argue between rows of wild-grown

    Bramblebush   Berryrash &   Garblegrass

    Rapeseed   Thornfester   *quack*

You, the Tinder-Poem:
The prairie grass is knee-high

Me, a literal rural goblin, still roosting in my Lady FemmeBoy Hooter Owlsona:
I think you mean ^me-high^

You sneeze, and that's all you have to say to that

The day boils away
We burgle yet another nap but this time in the hayloft of the filling station's
    livery stable

Two twenty-something year old boys
With Bart Simpson skateboards
    (Not him as a design on it but the board itself with the fin tail, that
    anachronistic
    barb troubling his otherwise fey immortal essence, you know?
    [A Simps-nonce, if you will]   [achoo])

They ride their gurgling skateboards thru the cobblestone parking lot of the
24/7 petro-manse of the evil sorcerer, Ir'Vyng

The surer one with the 5-panel hat and teal hoodie calls out something
unclear to the lithe one, lithe one with Ginsberg'ian receding hair and a plaid
button-down, frizzy and inquiring eh? and 5-panel reminding you'll need this,
handing over their shared, tired disposable face mask. Yeah I always forget about

these he says as he wraps his hand in it and thrusts his arm up to the elbow into the M ant icore door knocker's mouth, its inner sphere of annihilation, the sphere spurious and laughable in the face of a lickle bit of preparation, and the door swinging open with the usual curtsy of convenience store bell jangle jangle

I daydream of my lissome s'mores paladin AU alter-ego, Morley Ocher-Broil, who'll one day be rent real from nothing but magic and a bit of sugar by Swee Tooth the Mauve as a golem construct (we're still saving for the down payment), in deadly combat with the ultimate baddie:

> BBEG:
> *Just what do you think killing me will achieve*
> Me, but delicious and with a working body:
> *I think your blood will grease my blade, and so serviced, the blade shall do further great work, and with great alacrity.*

The snack-sumed boys sitting on the turtarrier looking up at us like they agree with Morley
Like they heard me

∴

Remember in *The Simpsons* when Abe Simpson called Apu "Achoo"?

Remember when punk-Itchy tricked cop-Scratchy[&a] into *skinning*[&b] himself?
Itchy chaining Scratchy's tail to a streetlight,
then taunting him and speeding away?

And then a pair of Itchy clones loaded Scratchy onto a plane for implied
  medical treatment?

But then you see the other passengers are The Big Bopper, Ritchie Valens, and
  Buddy Holly?

And you think "oh no this flight is doomed," but turns out that the punchline is
the three musicians bare their vampire[&c] fangs instead.

That joke is so slippery and polyphonic that it almost earns an honorary "queer"

Ye,

I too am haunted by the disappearance of the man in the opening credits
who ate a sandwich behind a sign
that said "be careful," who has been o'erwritten by Lenny and Carl with poor
ladder safety practices (*they actually overwrote gay-panic icons Smithers
and Burns unrolling schematics, the first to override anonymous luncher in
the early-middle Simpsons epoch)

We keep him in our hearts
Next to our Polly Pocket playsets
And our SIN cards

&a. ACAB, even the police-dogs, even the police-cats; you'll note there's no such thing as a police-rat

&b. Add one to the glossary, re: how to skin a cat

&c. It cannot fit here but we can't not somehow shoehorn in thoughts for, in in-world media akin to I&S, Blacula Meets Black Dracula,

where the titular vampires team up to contest forces which aim to turn their disco haunt into a hockey (honky, they cry out) rink

4. Habiliments

"The father of the boy who doesn't win / has to mow the [other's] lawn
in his wife's Sunday Dress."

—*The Simpsons*, s2e6

"Singin' hallelujah in the choir / To keep my feet out of the fire / My prairie
home / My prairie home / My prairie home / Fits like a Sunday Dress."

—Rae Spoon, *Sunday Dress*

∴

The fib erglass splinters in your father's hands are distracting the
congregation. They glimmer with work and anger and itch. They draw
attention to his callouses, to the omitted index digit, and the sable forked
tongue of the cleaved thumbnail, its cuticle a mauve rupt eyelid. The
congregation was distracted by this, and so they asked him to soak his hands
in the baptismal bowl at intermission (we are a progressive group, here), with
hopes the water would draw the fib erglass splinters from his hands. Those
most vocal surveil, scowl at the grease on his shirt cuff, the curdled purple
gunkhunk curled logy then loping in to fowl the holy wet mirror. But how
soft it makes his palm when he rustles your crown, your head buried by the
phonebook fog of multiplication tables. Those driven shards of light at the
threshold of his flesh, scared to death to find what comes next, listening for
the voice of god on the other side the door.

∴

BEING HEALED BY: CUMBATH

∴

The "you must be this tall to bathe in poesy" sign is written in the snowbank
    by a long fey
    French fry tusk
The fry salt melts a childish skip into the otherwise ornate timbre of the letters
The message can only be seen sometimes
When the sun tickles a glacial blue shadow from the plain white face of the snow

∴

—> yes, there is a poet that is just ever slightly "younger" and "fresher" than you close enough behind you to squish your shadow and they are reminding you that it's actually evil to say 'clean snow is good' because it is some obscure -*ism* they know and you don't (or you do know but didn't conspicuously let everyone else know you know), and that it's actually super disrespectful to write about a snow that's anything other than filthy and riddled with plastic waste [because *Dark Ecology*, which you want to point out is largely the same as a ton of Indigenous thought but don't point out because it hurts you to hurt others with knowledge (because you used to be very good at that)] which you *had* mentioned in an earlier published draft excerpt of The Repoetic with the dog shit, but when you messaged the younger poet about that they said that was "so suburban" of you, and sure, you'd always thought yourself trapped in an exurban condition (even though you grew up on a farm), but the point here is not to dwell on the fact that poets that might have been part of your generation (if "generation" wasn't a shrinking category with diminishing returns in an atomized bad neoliberal hellbroth world) are spineless (bad) cowards (okay, it's okay to be scared, just breathe) and don't know how to talk about work unless it's pity porn by marginalized writers (but of course they've never read that work even though they wield it like a cudgel) and they could've been your friend if they weren't traumatized into a mediocre competitiveness and they could've been your friend but you, you idiot poet, you are just a few too many memes behind the times. They're unhappy too, you see, there's this vicious jackal at their heels and they just don't know what to write about and don't want to get their first job ever before finishing their fully-funded phd on cumshit poetics; you get it. So, breathe: don't be a boob, bub.

∴

The starlight dyes the interstice static of the orators
We know it's a malfunction
But we're thinking of adopting it permanently

∴

A sterling untapped automat, right there, on the stroll to noneday whorlship
A bane on fane-face—but *the convenience*

A couple conceptualists have moved in down the lane
They wave at us, but evidently won't be attending service
They're writing poetry with microscopes and listeria bacteria, but everything
they do keeps coming out

"lady? full hysteria"

One day they'll master the copula, & then maybe the ant ecedents

In church a mumbleyodeling child keeps kicking the back of my seat:

thwap   thhhhwap

If this were a movie this would trigger a flashback to an airplane memory

But it takes a little more imagination than a pathetic winged tin-can can
muster to land a spot in The Repoetic

The Moff mutes his pre-recorded sermon a second, be-fanged and excited
to chastise the bored child, but fumbles his way instead to a lovely musique
concrete c ant ata, into applause, then disappears into the burp of night,
convinced by fear he'll never brush near that aplomb rapture 'gain

We recast him without noticing the difference, hecatomb rut, errata patch

    We recast him as a spell,
    as an ampersand,
    which contains itself,
    recurs in spellcast cursive.

Bugle—
    In my dreams
    Rockets buck ampers& rearview.

∴

thwap   *thwap*   *thwap*   *thwap*   *thwap*   *thwap*   *thwap*   *thwap*   *thwap*

thwap   *thwap*   *thwap*   *thwap*   *thwap*   *thwap*   *thwap*   *thwap*   *thwap*

thwap   *thwap*   *thwap*   *thwap*   *thwap*   *thwap*   *thwap*   *thwap*   *thwap*

thwap   *thwap*   *thwap*   *thwap*   *thwap*   *thwap*   *thwap*   *thwap*   *thwap*

thwap   *thwap*   *thwap*   *thwap*   *thwap*   *thwap*   *thwap*   *thwap*   *thwap*

thwap   *thwap*   *thwap*   *thwap*   *thwap*   *thwap*   *thwap*   *thwap*   *thwap*

thwap   *thwap*   *thwap*   *thwap*   *thwap*   *thwap*   *thwap*   *thwap*   *thwap*

thwap   *thwap*   *thwap*   *thwap*   *thwap*   *thwap*   *thwap*   *thwap*   *thwap*

thwap   *thwap*   *thwap*   *thwap*   *thwap*   *thwap*   *thwap*   *thwap*   *thwap*

thwap   *thwap*   *thwap*   *thwap*   *thwap*   *thwap*   *thwap*   *thwap*   *thwap*

thwap   *thwap*   *thwap*   *thwap*   *thwap*   *thwap*   *thwap*   *thwap*   *thwap*

thwap   *thwap*   *thwap*   *thwap*   *thwap*   *thwap*   *thwap*   *thwap*   *thwap*

thwap   *thwap*   *thwap*   *thwap*   *thwap*   *thwap*   *thwap*   *thwap*   *thwap*

thwap   *thwap*   *thwap*   *thwap*   *thwap*   *thwap*   *thwap*   *thwap*   *thwap*

thwap   *thwap*   *thwap*   *thwap*   *thwap*   *thwap*   *thwap*   *thwap*   *thwap*

thwap   *thwap*   *thwap*   *thwap*   *thwap*   *thwap*   *thwap*   *thwap*   *thwap*

thwap   *thwap*   *thwap*   *thwap*   *thwap*   *thwap*   *thwap*   *thwap*   *thwap*

thwap   *thwap*   *thwap*   *thwap*   *thwap*   *thwap*   *thwap*   *thwap*   *thwap*

thwap   *thwap*   *thwap*   *thwap*   *thwap*   *thwap*   *thwap*   *thwap*   *thwap*

thwap   *thwap*   *thwap*   *thwap*   *thwap*   *thwap*   *thwap*   *thwap*   *thwap*

thwap   *thwap*   *thwap*   *thwap*   *thwap*   *thwap*   *thwap*   *thwap*   *thwap*

thwap   *thwap*   *thwap*   *thwap*   *thwap*   *thwap*   *thwap*   *thwap*   *thwap*

thwap   *thwap*   *thwap*   *thwap*   *thwap*   *thwap*   *thwap*   *thwap*   *thwap*

∴

Okay okay so it's not illegal to ask someone why they don't celebrate their birthday
Sure
But we really recommend you quit it
Most of us can agree on that

∴

The whorl next door, who you once watched perform on a warbly old *whorls gone wild vol.666* VHS among a tamper-evident band of gruff dads (in alternate terms of venery, a khakis of dads), it's rumored whorl's been lately composing prose. Fortunately, those most maddened by her (really, by anything she does, horny or furious [usually both]) in our super-saturated cul-de-sac have been yet unable to assemble their IKEA guillotine, having lost the lone provided hex-key, owning no tools of their own

You remember her from a weekend babysitting certification seminar you took together (then still children both), thumb the expired, sun-kissed cert in the bloat obliviated Italian leather wallet gifted to you by your immortal mother in another lifetime, another whorld altogether

∴

"Where'd you come up with that?
"With what?
"That 'both' word.
"It's a nonce.
"Aha ha go to the corner and wear your nonce cap.
"No, a nonce cap is called a 'wimple.'

∴

The Hooters Owl in the Judas Hole but hasn't knocked yet
Hoo's there
Hoo's there?

This phosphorescent vole-vourer who hides in flesh so as not to suddenly
blind us; magnificent huntress, like all those whom man instinctively despises,
e'er collared with his frothing idiocy.

5. Tsundoku, or, Grubstake

"In The Repoetic everything will be perfect, while in our present prehistory the poem is never perfect and even when it would be, requires an effort that precisely implies an escape and denotes captivity."

—Saint-Pol-Roux, *La Répoétique*

"The Future is right now."

—Snake Plissken, *Escape from L.A.*

∴

...to the D-espair of earthly botanists, the trans-siD-ereal spectrum and ultra-munD-ane form and super-solar iriD-escence of an assiD-uous succorer slash sober sorcerer's Sacre-D Harp recital carpool, the rotun-D rotunD-a unD-er Her willow-shimmer all D-immer switch thumbe-D D-own naD-ir,

    & glut with spring pollen
    we all coo   *achoo*   as one.

∴

Hellbelch Re-D WenD-y's lighting keening thru the fog
Shiver with surety an upright swan-necke-D jackal-thing tro-D across your grave
That one D-ay will D-evour your unguarD-e-D molD-ering remains
That your strange sunD-ere-D boD-y is not sacre-D,
        especially not here among the many careering poets

∴

Pat D-own the many-voice-D "subversive" klaxon "inspirational" motet with a
    moist towelette

ah   quiet

Squeeze your eyes
HarD-er

Recall at start the automat athwart the fane, then untenante-D

∴

The monie-D ol-D poet whom no one likes an-D who is obsesse-D with
Esper ant o (there's n+1 of them in every cul-D-e-sac aroun-D the worl-D,
not just in The Repoetic) riD-es by on his bicycle, his cream specialty
D-iabetic socks upright gulpe-D up over his sweatp ants, pixel-pille-D
sweatp ants the brown of a never-tenD-e-D backyar-D plot's leaf-rot (a
colour one might easily imagine featuring prominently in a Go7 painting, all
CanaD-iana wilD-erness, nary an [Indigenous person] in sight); the gagging
socks sen-D a shiver D-own my spine, nostalgia riD-ing a bolt of lightning,
wherein I remember the stage-D boD-ies on pikes in *Cannibal Holocaust*, spear
in thru the bottom an-D out thru the mouth, eyes to heaven, so real looking
that the international community, for the most part at least, banne-D the
film, unclear on whether it was snuff or not; the basement we'-D watche-D
that in, after skateboarD-ing (baD-ly), after jamming (aD-equately), where
the milD-ew of "goo-D enough" (cause: a ne'er cleane-D D-ryer, e'er-wet)
always curle-D yr nose-hairs.

Those thoughts, just from some jerk's socks? This place really was a boon
for us unworthy wor-D-smiths.

The slick ol-D conlang-lovin' poet shouts "nice D-og, faggot" as he gliD-es
by, casual, bike veste-D with slight D-ecline momentum, no peD-aling, an-D
the fault long as a Ginsberg line in the concrete, though I know it's been
there a while alreaD-y, it almost seems to unspool from the man himself as
he cycles away.

∴

Chief Wiggum: "Geeze, how many gazebos D-o you shemales nee-D?"

Chuck GarabeD-ian: "That fancy yacht? A bargain 'cause it smells like cat pee. And those beautiful women? They use-D to be men."[&d]

MeD-itating on just what we've got on our hanD-s here. It's not errant, until like history it phoront hitchhikes from one inD-istinguishable suburb to the next. But it apes at errantry, an errant ant ambulating. Antagonistic, sometimes,
    in that it w ants to emboD-y err ant ry

TinD-er Poem been reminD-ing me lately not to forget to AD-D-ress the scientific D-iscovery, either, what we'-D thought was Einstein on the beach, but's time-slime on the beach

> Time-slime is a froth tie-D to the heaving of worD-s towar-D either *absolute present*, or *absolute immortality*, the salmon-hollanD-aise sickly yellow pink of the time-slime surf seems proof to me we're missing *the point*, D-upe-D both when plinth-ing present an-D when pretenD-ing we'll make something immortal while we're still enforcing 'phemeral borD-ers, while we're still sucking the petromarrow of the earth from the many petromancers' many pitte-D obsiD-ian reusable straws—*who D-rank my milkshake?*

Time-slime cannot be collecte-D for proper stuD-y, not even in a time-skein

Between the toes it gartersnake-snaps as a carbonate-D flicker but also as expecte-D, as a kin-D of grease, oil an-D water as it were, anathema to the san-D that woul-D otherwise worm in there, a kin-D of basic (in the alchemical, opposite-aciD-ic, sense) toe-jam, squelching with the spit-acoustics of what one imagines a brain hitting the pavement sounD-s like, ever-ether, splat slab bleater;

> up above the corkboar-D, several successive ble-D-out oilcans,
> PENN-LUBE IRVING—ING—ING—ING uglily ringing

Eager pleaser, oil-can [klepto/c'll'ct'r] geezer
what's our quart of law to D-ew with this reoffenD-ing litre?

D-ip yr quill in pen-lube an-D write your way out of this paper bag, why
D-on't-cha?

&d. From back to back episodes in May 1999. How many shithead Harvard grad dudes sitting in that writer's room were obsessed
with trans women, were hiring them for sex work, were stalking them and harassing them, wanted to be them (Daze says: "scrambled
eggs"), and then tried to sublimate their transmisogyny and other bullshit rich-kid hang-ups into stupid fucking jokes?

∴

    Imagine
D- aughter
D- ivine
D- i   D-   n't
D- o
    the
    saving
    of
    the
    scraps?

    Would
D- ivine
    hate
    how
    we
    seeme   -D
    to
D- rop
    the
    L
    in
    "Otherworl   D-   ly"

    only
    ever
    other/wor   D-   y

∴

Kefir-mustache making a man of you, the TinD-erPoem, in a way you sai-D
    a pronoun never D-i-D

The aD-obe Hooters' upstairs balcony railing ruste-D,
    a sanguine stain an-D verD-igris comet tail trailing
    from your clicky wrist ball to your D-ew-green grass-staine-D elb o /
    h / no
    coarse an-D col-D in the grounD-ing way

The system-reset escape-hatch reveals itself a lickle way off the property,
    where lawns lapse back into whorlD-erness

But so many merciless yanD-ere swans between us an-D promise-D no-poet bliss

∞ COD[V]A[MPIRES]

I am a vampire, I am a vampire
I have lost my mouth again

—Antsy Pants, "Vampire"

And all my friends were vampires
Didn't know they were vampires
Turns out I was a vampire myself

—Daniel Johnston, "Devil Town"

Then in the guise of cool air
In the softer hours he's there
Sitting talking in the voice of your mother
About leaving one good party for another

—Gord Downie, "Chancellor"

∴

We'd been pacing out front a long, long while. We'd done a home-invasion up the road, but the old fogeys hadn't even had gas to siphon in the tanks of their rickety old Jimmy SUV, their peach sun-kissed jerry-cans, and all the pills (nothing very sexy) in their medicine cabinet expired a few years ago; they'd been drowsing off there in their matching La-Z-Boy recliners, like they'd been waiting just for us to come finish them off. Dido found a couple blister packs of hearing-aid batteries that were the same juice our trunk-full-of-vibrators took though, so it wasn't a total bust.

The dragnet from the frustrated, thinned herd of locals was fast approaching. There were only so many range roads left to hide between. But then we saw it, caught its gilt glint. We stalked around alongside it a few days, unable to figure out a way in. We could all feel something was coming, it reeked, it rolled around on itself in the bedding of a many-month cast (Spike would've said it was "Effulgent"); it was virginity. But it wasn't a virgin-*who[re]*, it was a virgin-*where.*

We all felt it was about to come. We emerged from the punt-boats and the blinds at the sound of "and don't let the door hit your ass on the way out, faggot," and watched as a big hurricane-sonogram cum-spider horror and an overweight boy in an undersized Hooters cosplay outfit drooled into the reflection of an overlarge pocket mirror, pooling at first at the bottom lip of it, then Salchow'ing out, with a whoosh and gush like a lanced wound. The odd pair neglected to clasp the pocket-mirror's lid shut behind them, then ambled away through the stubble left by harvest.

When I was sure the odd couple were out of earshot, I approached the reflecting surface, of course not appearing, and I called out "any chance a couple wayward travelers might squeeze an invite from you? For a night or two?" That I couldn't see the world beyond the glass didn't mean it wasn't there, just as the fact I couldn't see myself in it didn't mean I wasn't here. And we got a meek "sure, who cares. No prose, though!" And that was good enough for us, those few who've honored chivalry and hospitality longer than any others living, or, less-than. We numbered one and nineteen more, and like any good guests, we shut the door behind us.

∴

Set to the withering "Dido's Lament" drooling from some unnamed ingenue's theremin: Nimble heteronyms scrambling for pole position in the himbo rankings, which did the one thing it wasn't supposed to do: brought them all together in likeness, but not, like, the Like Ness Monsters we immortals recognize those lessers to be [elusive, ever-ready for the imprint of a real personality (a podcast *didn't* count)]. Bromide and unicorn-hide. Puckish, peckish, peccadillo; prurient, with that same *rerr* as in *rural*, rural the "Crown Land" field we fled from (in)to this curious studio, this impossible landlocked island. This *Repoetic*, known elsewhere as Ratlantis, and sometimes the Balmderosa Ranch; only once so far as Fellowship of The Dreamt Universe. It is not a panacea nor samizdat (and don't listen to them if they tell you that). It lacks the strength of usual empire, weak like the light of the indehiscent glow-worm. It's bonnyclabber, charnel Parnassian, hapax legomenon, calque turion grown wild from untended tontine, and we, the observ ant undead, are those who'll collect on the forgotten wager.

∴

Rose wool hand-knit crop-top and pressed-felt ballcap (var.: backward), a lqqk what might not work were it not for vampire flaunting all that. Imagine it. That bit of chubby tummy, *yummy.* We vampires practically *invented polyamory,* but we certainly didn't go around bullhornily about it like the locals.

. . .

Yummy Amelia, reformed pilot turned vampiric mattress-actress, was getting too friendly with the clever locals, moaning things mid-blood-orgy like "let's tub this meeting," though Tony pointed out that might be closer to the way 'The Bard,' who he wouldn't shut the fuck up about having actually met the once, wrote.

"Just you wait" she'd smirk, smug with blood smeared on her cheek, just so, like she could blush. "This fun I'm having? It's catching."

The three of us cuddling close enough to squeeze into the lidded
        child-size coffin, one glaive's deep in the grave, one Danny Devito's
        wortha snow below the plowed berm

Rain eroding tippest tips of carrion's lingerfur into cog or sprocket or spurs
My perm pulling more than its hair-share of work around the delousing station

A street-dermatologist I used to pass past as one might Cassandra, or the
        homeless,
she wiped my pale right undertit with an acid tampon to scare away my ever-
        mole's shadow-moon
I had a brief night-dream of turning her, adding a fourth to our haptic hat-trick
        with comrade work-ethic
But then better sense came rage-caroling in like an ignored teapot

Reading Amelia's diary manifesto when she's sleeping the day away, while mole-
        anxiety keeps me awake:
•The kaleidostereoperoscope's panoptic prison holds many many multiprismners.
•Being agreeable isn't a personality these days.
•Unfortunately, neither is being disagreeable.
•A cool haircut CAN and WILL help.

So *that's why* she's been wearing the rat-tail lately

The exiled chose-coke poser's mother's acreage yard is pigeonholed with
    rarebirds (several snowy owls no less) because she leaves them the
    fuck alone, cuts her grass an angelic angle askew to that preferred
    by bordering golf course, bordering golf course (╯°□°)╯︵ ┻━┛'ing
    local rural water-table for its many jock-rot ball-wash stations; the
    exiled baron-administrator's mother is an immortal, supposedly, but
    not the way we are, and so we in our fear (and unlike the sociopathic
    trespassing bird-watchers), tend to keep our distance.

Thru th3 lampsick licks of light w3 thr33 robb3rs, smuggling candl3sticks
    (or w3r3 th3y just happy to s33 w3?) in hom3-s3wn robes, w3
    burglars whom row as on3 into th3 sho3 3mporium, sn3ak down
    sn3ak3r aisl3s qui3t as rabbit's pawsibl3, w3 slipp3rquipp3d rogu3s
    in shhstich custom gowns r3-r3alizing th3ir valu3 3ach succ33ding
    d3f3rr3d fir-grown st3p's groan on th3 way out th3 h3ist, counting
    thric3 to t3n to calculat3 our 3rd-y to3s' w3bb3d n3tworth

By the time the authorities pry us from our poached prize spyglass, our
    3go's adopted this vessel's form, a fat prefab thube of uncooked cookie
    dough leaking its raw egg ichor into the butcher's block—block cut
    awkward in the shape of a captain's tricorn.

The weight of the butcher's block is making it si-
    nk into our proffered child-size coffin honeymoon

· · ·

Caught by just a few of those many cops who don the guise of poets, we
men left Amelia behind to take the fall in the swoosh of track-jacket & the
surety of unspooling crime-scene gape, where these leftovers wear witness'
welcome thin, watching yet again the VHS-birth of The Repoetic as
forensick egregore vore f ant asy, a joke-rupt-by-hiccup haghounding its way
into existence twixt split sycamore Pocky sticks; Tone and me, triply lovesick,
& sick of it.

∴

We were all super sad that Rock Hudson was going to die so we begged (then 16 years old) Derek McCormack to turn him into a vampire and he did. We hid Rock away to protect him from all the horrible humans who said so many bad things about him now that they knew him as his lovers knew him, *a man among men*, but he got out in the middle of the night thru the kitchen's unclenched dog-door, and we haven't seen him since (though the trail of beautiful exsanguinated men might be a clue); we're happy to know he's somewhere out there, living afterlife to its fullest; we think he would've liked it here, generally overcast as it is.

∴

Dido was often complaining too many of the poets tasted like "kibble, like sawdust and butter." And Amelia too, that the one's pooled neck sweat had the tang of "the lost salt gift of blood," whatever that me ant.

At some point, one of the locals found our den in daylight hours, come by to ask to borrow some sugar. They tried to rouse the town-guard, *more like clown-guard*—more like *neighborehood-watch*—but the cathedral bell was catching a tan on the beach, broiling as only black cast-iron can. SO the poet smashed the next best thing, the proscenium's (more like *verscenium*) smitten gong, full-belt bellow, doe-eyed, doing it for [the Vine/Divine], tryna court the churlish centaur font necessary to lend the gravitas the warnin/g/ong needed: "there are vicious, needy things among us."

But that warning had seemed redundant to the rest of the poets, the kind of thing better left un-lineated. And when we vampires woke that night for Punk Rock Bingo, we cited our day-time exhaustion was due to "unusually high volumes of emotional-labour," in the tenor of the automated phone-operator that was t r a u m a; we vampires? we didn't come up with it, but we practically *perfected* trauma.

And so the knowing, warning poet drove herself quickly out of favour, *pariah par excellence*. And we, or at least those among us not dissatisfied with kibble et beurre, went back to our usual afterlives, struggling to straw-pierce the nigh impregnable octarine sanguine juice-pouches the magical automat provided us with when the herd was too thin to squeeze (which was rare, given just how many poets that lived here, seemingly no vetting process at all), standing around a single cellphone to remark on Amelia's latest OniFans post. Sure, sometimes we'd lose a few hours standing around talking about how we'd love to give Ames a 'sunrise surprise,' but of course, we had to spend all that time distinguishing between how that was funnier for vampires than it was for the mortal locals (it's a sign of respect to explain the joke back to the teller in our culture, to prove our understanding).

We weren't boring. We weren't missing the point. No matter what Dido's nightly negging implied. We knew how to have fun, like that time we slit the soy-boy's throat and with it soy-soaked the popular "translator's" backyard rooibos crop on Roanoke Dr., cackling like kids at a burst hydr ant in the zenith of summer, unable to help ourselves, or at least, like we *imagine* kids in the bacchanal sun would comport themselves, given our wretched collective memory and usual s[ome/un]time sensitivities.

∴

The poets are the haemohegemony, and we are the counter-culture, but counter like the first math—addition: *vannn misguided diatribe from a middle-class cultural enforcer who's hogging everyone else's trauma like it's the only fully functioning N64 controller at the party, twooo misguided diatribes from middle-class cultural enforcers who're hogging everyone else's trauma like they're the only two fully functioning N64 controllers at the party, three,* and so on and so forth (tho' this metaphor only goes to four) *[wah] [ah] [ah] [!]*

Throw down your wedding rice and we're obliged to count it, and to start over in the middle when the pigeons get at it. Same for your iambs. Cast your morphemes into apocalipsick word mattes and we will dutifully untangle them, and as such prattle-wranglers, we re-arrange (though never to our satisfaction) *a multiplicity of tiny, fragmented regions in which nameless resemblances agglutinate things into unconnected islets,* will hank your skein then force its rhyme. We bare our hearts and fangs entwined.

∴

A tragedy: the most recent potluck housewarming in the cul-de-sac, some normie poet bit our ring-giver on the neck while ring-giver was just warming up his mesmerism, the horny poet too impatient to nurse a hickey like anyone with any sense might. It shocked our leader so surely that he didn't bite the poet back. He woke up the morning after a human, a boring human with nothing worth saying at all but a real thirst to do so; a kind of inside-out vampire.

His condition has been deteriorating. At first, he'd just stay up late to join some others for boozy brunches. A depressed, FOMO-laden former vampire with unbrushed orangefangs drinking a bit of beer on the patio, the bit of gold foam mountain-capping each undertusk like candy corn. His fangs hadn't gone away, or not that we could tell—Dido, the only reasonable one among us, had likened their erosion to that of mountains, that we were thinking too lively in our temporality, forgetting the actual span we were so blessed with, our true temporal (ad)v ant age—and so we'd been lying to ourselves, thinking those 'lasting' Cheeto fangs fomenting omens of a fuller, deathly recovery.

But soon enough the dementia set in, his body having lingered so long in the world, unsure how to recalibrate now to this re-boot post-post-life crisis—especially in this unreal place, this pocket-mirror mirror-verse made of nothing but clever quips and a desire to better know one another—his vitality's deferral called in even though the deferral had initially been a polite way of saying "nah, I'm out, but thanks for the opportunity."

This morning he woke up with the sun and smelled his palms, ripe now with yesterday's nutty somethin' or other Body Butter, but he couldn't remember, he couldn't figure which rings went onto which fingers.

And so, in his embarrassment,
he's given the-
m all away

∴

Lady Di was going on again about diversity initiatives and how Nimbus Terrafaux was our only POC in our little artery. But NT was so aloof. He didn't seem to *identify* with the rest of us at all. Hell, I don't think he and I have ever shared more than a few words at the blood-brunch buffet. And then those cucks, Dido and Amelia, backed Lady Di's diversity nonsense up. We're a secret-group of bloodsuckers: we don't need a *visible diversity* initiative; that's contrary to our wellness: self-care first, your own mask then the others, all that. We need to blend in, but given our usual asocial, discreet scripts, we actually stick out more for our not incess ant ly interjecting as the locals do; a few of us have started writing some lines even, but we're terribly out of fashion (I cannot write a sonnet about Anacondas, sestinas about DOTA2). Di, Dido and Amelia were downvoted during the sire-pyre BBQ [it used to be a potluck, 'til they got all PC about that shit too (not that any of them qualified what was wrong with it, just snapped at it and failed to engage when I asked if they'd meant 'powwow')]. Me and the rest of the boys are thinking of turning Kenneth Goldsmith instead; we liked that bit he did with Killary's emails, printing them out like that. You need that kind of sense of humour, when yer gonna live forever.

∴

SHIT SHIT SHIT! He was going to be late, again

A blur in his peripheral as he rushed by, on the indie-theatre marquee:
SUPERVAMP D-LUXE, 1925

Scrambling then stub-toe ambling away from the ambit of the sold-out automat—sold-out short a single nearly-expired juice pouch of AB négati[f/ve], there for the taking, for anyone with the cash (he didn't have the cash; he wished, but he was committed to it, he was living the impoverished life of the "true poet")—the sunscreen-slathered virtue-signaling pseudo-vegan human-wannabe vampire was gonna be late for his seminar the second week in a row, and Dr. Formal (née D.Hyde) hadn't liked last week's stab at sestinas.

The wannabe simply couldn't think up better words for the envoi than

1. OCTARINE (oh how he loved how clever Terry Pratchett and Neil Gaiman were)
2. SANGUINE (yum)
3. GUSH (oh it dripped with erotic energy, didn't it? Though Dr. Formal disagreed)
4. CUM (duh!)
5. RED (it let him pun on *reading* too, which he'd been so sorely wrong would get him at least a few points on the vague and slippery rubric Dr. Formal refused to disclose)
6. and last but not least, BITE (he'd f ant asized of Dr. Formal describing his work as having "bite," but instead got critiqued as producing writing that was "quite toothless")

To top things off, he'd forgotten his trusty IBM pocket-protector this morning, and his Judas-fucking blood-glut quill (he was going for a kind of spooky *Poe*-sian aesthetic, coming up poser for the most part) was bleeding down onto his chest, blood blotting the gingham cotton above his ticklish right nipple, then around it, rung 'round now and looking not unlike a pacifier, a pacifier for the piteous idiot baby the wannabe-normie vampire was and always would be:

AND THIS IS WHAT YOU GET FOR W ANT ING TO BE
        DIFFERENT THAN YOU ARE,
THIS IS WHAT YOU DESERVE.   kidding :p   (sparag/mos/tly)

Did[c]o[detta]

"And even if I'm there, they'll all imply
That I might not last the day"

—Dido, "Thank You"

∴

th rill pl ant ed   Gr ant b rill i ant   X ant hus   gr
    ant ed   w ant on Garam ant ian   gr ant ed m ant les pleas ant ants
    gr ant   gr ant ed Bacch ants'   w ant   exult ant fr ant ic

sl owl y owl
c hoo se false hoo d

love-pang   love   love's   love-enkindled   love   loved   love
    love   lovers lovely   love   lover   love   love
    loved   love   Love   love   lover   love   love   love
    lovers   love   love   lover

woman woman woman's woman woman's women's woman

her breast   opened breasts her breast   comely breast   her
   breast   her breast

wh en   wh at   Wh o   wh o   wh at   Wh at   wh o   wh o
       wh om wh ose W hy Wh at wh at wh at wh ile
       wh ile wh ite wh at wh ile wh ich wh en wh at
       wh at   Wh y   Wha t Wh o   wh ether *wh* at w *orl* d
       wh ile wh ole Mean wh ile Wh en wh en wh ile
       Wh en Mean wh ile wh o   wh om wh ile wh om
       wh en   wh o   wh om wh ile wh o   *wh* o   w *orl* d
       Wh at   what wh ich wh o   wh ose wh ile wh ole
       wh ich wh im wh o   Wh at wh at wh om wh ile
       wh at   wh at Wh at mean wh ile wh o   wh en
       wh en   Wh at! wh ich wh ose wh y   *wh* ose f *orl* orn
       wh ile wh ile wh y   wh om wh ile wh ole wh y
       wh at   wh ile wh o   Wh at Wh at No wh ere *whirl* ed
       wh en   every *wh* ere w *orl* d wh en Wh at wh at
       wh ole wh at Wh y   Wh ither   wh ich wh ich,

wh en   wh en   wh ich   *wh* enever   w *orl* d   f *orl* orn
wh en   wh o   wh ile   wh en   wh ere   wh o   wh om
wh ile   wh en   wh en   wh en   wh at   wh atever
wh en   wh en   wh at   wh om   wh o   Wh at   wh om
wh en   wh ile   wh oever wh iten

Wh at say I?   Wh ere am I?   Wh at madness turns my brain?

wh en   wh o   wh om   wh ole   wh ose   wh ose   wh en   wh enever
         a wh ile *wh* ile   F *orl* orn, wh at   wh en   wh atever
         wh en   underw *orl* d

Dido herself   Dido burns   Dido was   Dido is   Dido plan
    Dido and   Dido and   Dido swayed   Dido deigns
    Dido had   Dido knows   Dido? Even   Dido's name
    Dido, at   Dido prays   Dido, do   Dido, trembling

Acknowledgements

• To listen to the OST for this curious book, go to:
https://bonnyboy.bandcamp.com/album/the-repoetic-ost.

• The poem is a "reboot" of Saint-Pol-Roux's *La Répoétique*, a 'lost' mid-century long-poem, fragments of which were published posthumously by Rougerie in the 1970s (fragments rescued by his daughter, Divine). While I have worked to translate SPR's work to satisfy my own curiosity, this poem (the one yr holding, perhaps have thrown thru a window in frustration) was generated as a kind of detritus, a shadow-text parallel to that original project, and is a wholly original new work. I found the ur-poem originally as a brief mention within the joyous account about 'error' by American Surrealist Franklin Rosemont, *An Open Entrance to the Shut Palace of Wrong Numbers*, purchased for me by Evan Winstanley, while we were stupid teenagers and very fucking lost in Boston and warming from a downpour in some musty anarchist bookshop; thank you, E.W., for this lasting gift. While I would love to one day better 'perform' Roux's own original utterance of what a Repoetic might look like, I admit I am, to quote Elliot Page in Juno, plainly "ill-equipped."

• "*Mara Jade-d*" references dickhead Nick Land but only to turn over the problem of the left's usual ouroborosian self-defeating melancholy, but it more nourishingly references Stuart Ross' poem "Tengo Fuengo," from the b rill i ant "Farmer Gloomy's New Hybrid," a copy of which was gifted to me by the too-kind and also b rill i ant Hugh Thomas, to whom I am grateful for his mentorship and friendship. An earlier version of this piece was published in *NōD Magazine* Issue 28.

• "Marilyn Gorgonroe…" comes from a day-dream about Dropout.TV's Dimension 20, specifically the highly-lethal season of D&D "A Crown Of Candy" wherein various Candy-Land-esque people fought to prevent all-out war; Ally Beardsley's backup character (each player had one, given the high lethality), who they didn't need to play in the end, was a "s'mores knight" named Sir Amanda Maillard. My obsession with characters that *don't quite exist* extends to "Lady Di was going on again…," where I name Nimbus Terrafaux, a prank by a gaming magazine about how everyone was obsessed with hidden Mortal Kombat characters, as one of the vampires in the nest. I suppose those few named & noble vampires in the batch are folks I wish had been 'saved,' or 'made realer,' in one way or another.

• "...*Tag yrself: yr 'canada beef inc'*" draws from digital correspondence with American poet Hazel Avery, who is one of my favourite poets.

• "The Hooters Owl in the Judas Hole but hasn't knocked yet..." garbles a hard mistranslation of a piece of Roux's original, specifically a passage in "AGE-OF-THE-SUN or FUTURE WORLD."

• "...to the D-espair of earthly botanists" garbles and reconfigures some mondegreen phrases I misheard when being read to by a friend from the beloved purple prose of ur-spook-clerk, Clark Ashton Smith.

• "'Chief Wiggum...'" recalls Bishop's "Filling Station," whose grease-stained barbs cannot be safely extracted from my brain, and thus I have set out to domesticate as best I can.

• "We'd been pacing out front a long, long while..." references Marty Robbins' iconic "Big Iron."

• "Dido was often complaining..." features the gag "OniFans," which I first heard on video-game streamer (then-named, and I think changed by publication of this poem) ItsGreedyy's *Dead By Daylight* streams, which were a great comfort to me during the long labour-intensive recovery of my dog Bacchus (attacked by two off-leash king shepherds—one of whom I had to fucking knock out to get it to let go of him—Bacchus lucky to have made it out alive), when I had no other means of entertainment, exhausted, naïve and hopeful the forthcoming spring would bring health and a return to socialization (instead, we got what we got, and I'd rather not name it here, a kind of literary tinnitus from the word buzzing in my brain); Sebastian's streams seemed at that time delivered by some blessed stork-like-algorithm, and while I know the parasocial is a poisonous wretched marketing scheme (or it can be and usually is), at the end of the day, sitting around with my doped up, sleepy, healing dog on my lap, watching someone happily play video-games and interact with a chat geared to good-will was just the soul-balm I needed at the time. "Kefir-mustache making a man of you..." also references the DBD mechanic of an end-game hatch used to escape the killer. "*BEING HEALED BY: CUMBATH*" is also found text from one of Greedyy's streams, as a fellow DBD player, username "cumbath," performed the heal action on Greedyy's own avatar. The world writes its own poetry and it's not always better than what we come up with but probably it is better 99% of the time.

• "The poets are the haemohegemony..." quotes Foucault's *The Order of Things*, a bit surrounding aphasiacs written in service of the elliptical near-definition of 'heterotopia.'

• "th rill pl ant ed..." is lathed from Book 4 of *The Aeneid*, from a translation by Henry Rushton Fairclough, described at a cursory Google as "an American classical philologist of Canadian ancestry," which, well, it sounds like he was great at parties lmao. This translation was freely pasted on the web, and riddled with spelling errors, which I think is what makes it really real; I was not going through my stored books to find whatever translation of it I already owned. There is no incredible Oulipo secret to what I've done here. I just looked for whatever sonic bits I liked and yanked them out in the order they appear in the original. The choice to couple instances of "Dido" with its immediately following words was arbitrary: because I wanted to. That the exhausting stanza trying to cleave 'wh- -orl's together also brings in a bunch of homophonic hoo hoo'ing to tie to the preceding owl-motif / hoo reference is a happy accident. And no, this isn't the Dido from the Eminem song. But I'm not gonna make that 'canon' either. Hell, you know what? It's both Dido-s now, if you're thinking of the same two I am. Fuck it I'll make her famous song, the one Eminem samples, the epigraph even. Wow that's cute. So clever. Okay everything is canon if you want it, have at thee, faces which launch a thousand ships and thousander fan-fics.

• With thanks to: kelly hill (+Caro & Judith), Avi Diggle, N.Page, William Seto Ping III, Rudi Aker, Tom D. Wilson, Patrick O'Reilly, Lisa Banks, Keane Wiebe, Emily V.H., Jim Johnstone, Jami Macarty, Triny Finlay, Mark Anthony Jarman, Andreae & Mark Callanan, Rebecca Salazar, Katie Fewster-Yan, Clay Everest, Mel McMichael, Jeff Arbeau, Mable Munroe, Oliver MacPhee, Ry2K/J.Acreman/K.B., Justin LeClair, Daze Jefferies, Hazel Noisette, Miriam Richer, Allison Calvern, John Colasacco, Jesse Eckerlin + Kess Mohammadi, Eel Eye W., Lisa Moore, Fiona Pollack, Karen Solie, and my whole family. Blame these people if you hate this book, as they clearly didn't try hard enough to stop me from being bad at poetry so long that I kind of got good at it.

Also to: everyone I foolishly forgot or menacingly and quite purposefully omitted as an aggressive-aggressive fuck you!

And also to: Shane, and everyone else at Gordon Hill Press for publishing things that don't readily pour into the familiar decoy molds of CanLit, and for reading my work so swiftly and generously.

Lastly to: Bacchus, dog of longest eyelash, stubborner than even my immortal mother.

About the Author

Benjamin C. Dugdale is a poet & experimental filmmaker currently living in Rural Alberta (Treaty 7 territory). B's writing can be found in places like *GEIST, Plentiude, Riddle Fence, giallo, filling station*, &c., and their films have screened across the globe at festivals such as Sick 'n' Wrong, Videodrunk, Gotta Minute, Bideodromo, and London Experimental. B also reads for *PANK* and *ARC Poetry*, and sometimes publishes as bonny CD. Their updates can be found at benjamindugdale.ca. Their debut chapbook, *Saint Rat O'Sphere's Formica Canticle Poems*, was published in 2020 by Anstruther Press, and their most-recently completed experimental film project, *Contents Under Pressure*, is distributed by the CFMDC. *The Repoetic: After Saint-Pol-Roux* is their debut full length poetry collection.